Race Track Attack Guide

Auto Club Speedway

The Enthusiast's Approach to the High Performance Driving Experience on America's Road Racing Courses

Edwin Reeser, III

Sericin Publishing Company

Copyright 2010, Sericin Publishing Company

All rights reserved. World rights reserved. No part of this book may be reproduced in any form or by any means, electronic or mechanical, including photocopying, recording or by any information storage and retrieval system, without the prior written permission of Sericin Publishing Company, except in the case of brief passages embodied in critical reviews or articles.

ISBN Number: 978-0-9841724-3-6

Library of Congress Control Number: 2010906169

DISCLAIMER: The contents of this book are true to the best knowledge of the author. All recommendations are made without guarantee on the part of the author or the publisher. The author and the publisher disclaim any liability incurred in connection with the use of any data or recommendations in this book. In particular, no portion of this book should be taken to suggest or condone the violation of any traffic laws or the practice of any unsafe driving.

Printed in the United States of America

All maps used to illustrate the Auto Club driving lines are from Matthew Reeser and Kathryn Marcellino.

All photos are from Edwin Reeser.

A publication of Sericin Publishing Company, Sericin Management, LLC.

Matthew Reeser, Editor in Chief

Contents

Foreword 5
Introduction 9
The Track 13
Perspective 19
Track Entry 27
The Roval of Turns 1 and 2 33
Turns 3 and 4 43
Turns 5 and 6 51
Prepare for the Unexpected 55
Turns 7 and 8 63
Turn 9 65
Turn 10 69
Turns 11 and 12 73
Turn Segments 13, 14 and 15, 16 77
Turn 17 83
After Turn 17 to the Front Straight 87
Track Exit 93
Distinguishing Characteristics 97
Conclusion 99
Closing Note on Driving Lines 101
Track Checklist 103
Tech Inspection Checklist 107
Dedication 109
Acknowledgement 111
About the Author 112
Other Race Track Attack Guides 113

Foreword

It is a pleasure to be able to "begin" this work of Ed's. Through years of racing, and serving as board member and then Regional Executive (RE - CEO) of the California Sports Car Club ("Cal Club", the Southern California region within the Southern Pacific Division of the SCCA that also includes, Southern Nevada, Arizona and Hawaii), I have spent many hours at Auto Club Speedway (Cal Speedway for those of us who have trouble with name changes). Cal Club is the oldest and most storied racing club in the West, the historic home of road racing, and presently holds two events a year on this big, fast speedway. That means lots of time on this course.

When Riverside International Raceway gave way to a shopping mall, we lost that historic and special race place in the center of our community. Fortunately, we are blessed with several wonderful race tracks in our region, including Buttonwillow, Willow Springs, and now Chuckawalla Valley. All of these are at least a couple of hours tow from where most of our members live. So it was a blessing on the tow budget when centrally located Cal Speedway opened its doors in Fontana, California. Renamed the Auto Club Speedway, this is a first class facility, but one that is a true challenge.

Often times road courses built within or as part of an oval race course can have an artificial feel, and may lack the technical aspects which make track time so much fun and such a learning challenge. Not the case with Auto Club Speedway, where the first class nature of the facility is felt on track too.

Anyone interested in performance driving (PDX/HDPE) will find this book required reading before putting one wheel on this challenging track. Those in the wheel to wheel racing community know how difficult, and to be frank... intimidating, this course can be. Ed's efforts have provided a way to avoid pitfalls and safely improve your times, improve your skills, and raise the fun meter to the highest levels by carefully following his counsel.

I once was talking to Andy Porterfield about the speed I was maintaining in my American Sedan (Ford Mustang) through NASCAR 1 and 2 (Ed calls that the ROVAL). I was over 150 mph and frankly it worried me. I was "breathing the motor" with an ease of throttle – and it was hard to keep my foot down. So I went to Andy and asked him what was he doing through NASCAR 1 and 2? Andy told me that in his GT 1 car he was over 175 mph – and it was hard to keep his foot down. When

FOREWORD

Andy Porterfield says it is a challenge, then every one of us lesser beings should feel encouraged to accept the reality of Auto Club Speedway - it is a challenge, and not just there! (I note here that Andy Porterfield was 25 mph faster through that corner than the CUP cars – but of course the GT 1 has bigger tires, is much lighter, a different suspension and has a Cup motor in it. Then you put a driver of Andy's caliber in it, and it is no mystery as to why it is FAST.)

Reading and then re- reading this book is like having a professional instructor in your car all the time, but without the extra weight. This Race Track Attack Guide-Auto Club Speedway should be mandatory reading for all who venture out on this race course for PDX, Time Trials, and Track Days. As Ed points out so very well, this can be a dangerous activity, but with his solid counsel, your study, practice, preparation and effort the rewards are great. What is more, everything – and I mean everything – we learn on the track makes us better and safer street drivers if we allow it to be so.

So study this book, listen to the instructors, practice, practice, practice and move the fun meter up the scale. You will be rewarded on several important levels.

A round of applause for Ed and his efforts.

    Steve Staveley
    Regional Executive-CEO
    California Sports Car Club
    Southern Pacific Division, SCCA

Turn 13-14 combination at the end of the infield straight requires late entry to Turn 13 to stay on stripes at right edge on corner exit.

Turn 14 entry is now opened up to wider arc for faster exit transition into Turn 15.

Auto Club Speedway

Introduction

Added to the inventory of road racing courses in the United States in 1997, Auto Club Speedway is a well groomed and modern facility. Host to NASCAR and other popular professional racing events, the facility is well equipped and conveniently located to a large number of driving enthusiasts, just sixty miles east of downtown Los Angeles on Interstate 10, then one mile north at the Cherry Avenue exit.

There is seating for 92,000 fans, parking for 32,000 cars, and all the amenities one could hope for as an enthusiast driver, including three spacious garage buildings with 100 car spaces and work benches for equipment, electrical outlets for power tools, large and clean bathrooms, a selection of leaded and unleaded high octane racing fuels, a driver's room with video screens, white boards for meetings and instruction, etc.

This Track Attack analysis will take the driver through one of the more challenging road courses in the western United States, a counterclockwise lap of the 2.8 mile, 20 turn auto competition course configuration at Auto Club Speedway in Fontana, California. Many of the turns at Auto Club Speedway are compound corner configurations of two or more, or otherwise merit consideration and analysis together as segments, and that is how we will explore them for this track.

One should always do a track map study of a circuit before driving the course, view in car videos, look at still photographs of corners and features, and even play a video game simulation, as well as talk to drivers and instructors well experienced with the track. However, none of these will adequately convey the sensory sensations from the extraordinary rush of air and sound from the engine and tires reverberating off the track wall as you hurtle down the 11 degree banked curving front straight, below grandstands that seat tens of thousands of spectators, at wide open throttle in top gear, the lateral g forces of the high speed sweep through the 14 degree, 75 foot wide banking of Turns 1 and 2, the deceleration pressure on the chest through application of hard braking and four gear drops to shed almost 100 mph of speed before making a sharp turn in to the compound pair of double 90 degree Turns 3 and 4, the yaw/rotation/countersteering in the double apex 180 degree horseshoe of Turns 5/6, "threading the needle" of the high speed chicane of Turn 7/8, picking the correct braking line and two gear drops through Turn 9 to set up the proper corner entry point for the hard right hairpin of Turn 10, a WOT charge through the chicane of Turns 11 and 12 and down the infield straight, followed by thresh hold braking and two gear drops to a three corner compound right-left-left turn combination of Turns 13, 14, and 15, aligning the nose of the car in Turn 16 to make a sharp, narrow left 110 degree turn with tire walls on the right side in Turn 17, and then picking a smooth line through the linked series of right to left bends commencing with Turn 18 to allow maximum speed at entry to the front straight and a foot to the floor blast in top gear that may be the fastest and longest sustained wide open throttle segment of any road racing track in the West.

There is speed, braking, car control and technique challenge all over this course. And more than a few concrete walls. Under proper supervision and sponsorship, this course is accessible to most drivers at this writing.

Exit from Turn 6 presents good opportunity for a safe pass before chicane of Turns 7-8.

After exit from Turn 12, transition from right edge to left edge on infield straight, and prepare for two or three gear downshift under braking.

The Track

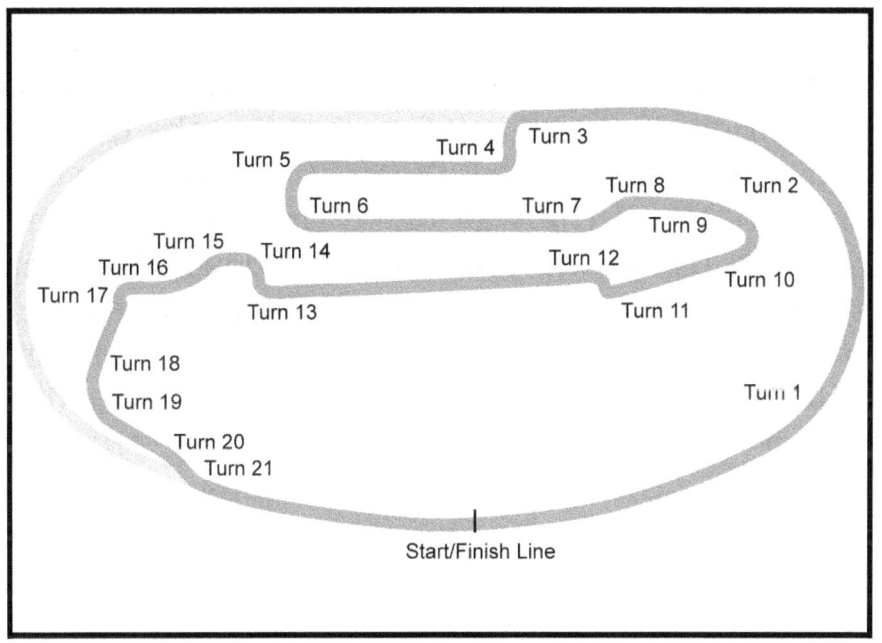

While a chance to drive any car on a race track is usually great fun, that might not be the case at any track absent a well organized event, and the great majority of event sponsors at Auto Club Speedway fortunately attend to this carefully. Before selecting your event sponsor to run with at California Speedway, be sure you confirm that they follow a disciplined safety orientation for all drivers, clear rules, and rigorous adherence to those rules.

The auto competition layout is as well designed and "safe" as a road racing circuit may inherently be... but it still presents risks associated with concrete K - rails, perimeter walls, and stacks of tires, coupled with some of the highest speeds to be experienced on any circuit in the US, especially for the more powerful cars. A normally aspirated Miata is going to give "giddy up" fits to the driver on this track configuration, not to mention cramps in the right foot and calf from holding the throttle pedal to the floor for a 5,000 foot run from the exit of Turn 17 all the way on to the front straight, through the Roval, and part way down the back straight and entry to Turn 3. A high horsepower car will have the driver experiencing circulatory challenges from the waist down to the ankles due to excessive cheek clench the first few times though the banked turns. The "Roval" run down that long front straight and through the banked Turns 1 & 2 is an experience like no other for most road course racers, and demands serious attention to safety, both mechanical for the car and mental for the driver.

Many high performance cars off the showroom floor have the capacity to reach velocities in excess of 160 mph on that front straight, and modified street cars and exotics to 180 mph or more... and this makes preparation of suspension, aerodynamics and handling, and driver skill, a much greater matter of concern compared to many tracks where brief attainment of 130 mph in a straight line once per lap is likely to be the best one can coax out of their machine. A comparatively minor glitch at 80 mph can be catastrophic when experienced at 150 mph, and when you confront that challenge at such high speeds once or twice per lap, ten or twelve laps per session, five sessions in a day... both you and your equipment are in harm's way fifty to one hundred times... and had best be properly prepared.

That does not make the preparation any different than what you should do for any track day experience... just perhaps a bit deeper and more respectful. Fully understand the limits of your equipment and yourself before you hit the grid at Auto Club Speedway.

For the stock set up, and intermediate to advanced level driver at the wheel experiencing the Roval on his or her own for the first time, (and no matter what your experience level, you should take a right seat ride a few times around before you take this circuit behind the wheel on your own, and also do it at the wheel with an instructor by your side), a corner entry velocity of the lesser of what you think you are comfortable with based on your driving experience and skills, the equipment's capability, and certainly no more than 125 mph, is what you should consider. As with all corners, take it slowly at first and work your way up in carefully considered increments of speed.

One difference with the Roval is that if you spin you don't necessarily wind up backwards in a cloud of tire smoke, or ten feet off the asphalt in the grass and dirt, like one does on many road courses... but caroming off a concrete wall at triple digit speed. So use your head to think through your set up and approach before you climb into the car. Leave the ego at home when you go to Auto Club Speedway to drive the Roval.

(Beginner's note: The Roval is probably the safest turn on the course for the novice who is with an instructor. It is seventy five feet wide, banked fourteen degrees and smoothly paved, and you just keep the speed down and the car under control. The challenge for you will be to focus on the proper driving line and keeping your field of vision up, as there is a tendency to pull your line of sight closer down off the nose of the car and to then suddenly look back up... at the wall... and drive right up the banking into it.

The car has a tendency to go where you are looking, a somewhat instinctive coordination between your vision and your hands, so keep your focus and vision directed where you want to go, not necessarily where the nose of the car is pointed at any moment in time. Swivel your head to the left slightly and follow the driving line. For the rest of the track, concentrate on properly identifying the apex of your infield corners and work on identifying and following your driving line, braking points, turn in points and other essential skills.

Just cruise, do not challenge, through the Roval and enjoy the thrill of driving where the NASCAR legends drive.)

Do not be dismissive of the repeated emphasis in this analysis on high speed issues associated with this circuit, as the purpose is to help you know where to focus to manage that speed. Going fast, and going fast *safely,* are not the same thing. Any person, and many trained animals, can get behind the wheel of a powerful car, hold the wheel straight and put the accelerator to the floor.

You must not mistake the capabilities engineered into the car to be an extension of your capabilities as a driver, especially with respect to car control at speed. Having a fast car and being a fast driver are two unrelated statements of fact.

Driving this course is terrific fun, but you must recognize and respect the limitations of the track, the car, and yourself with clarity. While most beginners approach track days with the reserve and caution appropriate to reduce risk of mishap, there still are places where a modest mistake at slow speed, such as an early apex into Turn 10 or 17, can put the car into the grass or a stack of tires. For the intermediate and advanced drivers who are pushing the envelope of performance limits for their cars, and their own driving skills, but at higher speeds than they may be used to, the Roval must be respected, and car control through 13/14/15 can be a challenge. Control recovery at high speed is more difficult, and the consequences of lost control to man and machine more severe with concrete walls, so respect this attribute of speed when driving Auto Club Speedway.

Even a slow speed corner such as Turn 17 can put the driver into a tire barrier. Resist the temptation to creep left before corner entry. Hold steadily to the right edge of the surface until making a late turn in.

Perspective

Reality Check: Before we get into how to enjoy High Performance Driving Education ("HPDE") and the track notes for the Auto Club Speedway, a few words about what this experience is about and its risks.

Many sports involve highly developed skills where you throw, catch, strike, or kick a ball. If you make a mistake the result typically involves a lost point, a change in possession, a replay, or perhaps a lost ball and a "do over" with a scoring penalty, and the game continues. In *high performance driving, you are the ball, and there are no second chances*. Accordingly, driving the "ball" over the fence or into the lake is not an option.

Some sports have a significant potential of serious injury or death if things go wrong. You may do everything right yourself, and still get caught by the mistakes of others or unpredictable events. Mountain and free climbing, scuba diving, sky diving, spelunking, bungee jumping, hang gliding, bull fighting and driving a car, motorcycle or bicycle fast all can have seriously negative consequences, irrespective of fault. If introducing even a moment of inattention to a relatively safer activity, such as crossing a street on foot, can be fatal, (stepping into the path of a bus while reading the morning paper, for example) then it is clear that a moment of inattention in one of the aforementioned activities is potentially more so.

All sports require a detailed level of knowledge and practice to perform well. Striking a golf ball is not an inherently natural series of coordinated actions. Neither is throwing, catching or hitting a baseball, climbing the face of a rock wall, or making a controlled sky diving free fall. HPDE driving is most definitely an undertaking that benefits from serious study of the geometry of tracks, the components and working of your car, the art of driving, safety considerations at all levels, and physical and mental preparation of the driver. You will drive better and be safer if you devote the time and energy to do it right by studying, and practice.

Driving a car is an inherently dangerous activity. Driving a car fast, even under the best of conditions and preparation in a well-controlled track situation, is even more so. A 3000 pound car moving at 60 mph has the potential energy to move a 5,808 TON block of concrete one foot. That car moving at 120 mph has the energy to move a 23,232 TON block of concrete one foot. A speed of 120 mph is not really "fast" in the auto racing world. There are numerous circuits where a street car can reach speeds of as much as 150 mph, or more. **Auto Club Speedway is one of those tracks**. As kinetic energy increases as the square of speed, twice as fast means four times the energy. If there is a problem on the street or the track, all that energy has to go someplace before your car comes to a stop. If it is dissipated through braking to a smooth stop it is highly desirable, as contrasted with a series of violent roll over strikes upon the ground or against a concrete wall. This is especially true if the concrete wall does not move and the energy is absorbed by the compression of the car with _you_ inside of it.

As you spend more time on the track, the odds of having an unpleasant experience will tend to catch up with you. You will exit the track surface, lose control of your car or have someone lose control of their car in front of you. All people make errors in judgment. All things mechanical and electrical can and eventually will break or fail. Random events can and do suddenly occur. They have happened to me, and all of the other drivers that I know, so there is no reasonable expectation that you will escape this fundamental reality any more than you can defy the laws of gravity.

But you can prepare to make the best of it when bad things happen. Part of the focus of this book is to bring to light how you approach driving and maintaining your car, and whether you may need to consider changing your approach to make yourself a safer driver on the street and track. You may find that track experience can benefit you on the street, keep you out of trouble. Not because you can drive faster than others, but because you are more aware, have developed additional car control skills, and can get the most out of your car and yourself in an emergency.

If you cannot accept the responsibility or consequences of driving on a race track, don't do it. Driving a car under the laws applicable in all licensing jurisdictions that I am aware of is not a right, it is a privilege, and you are responsible to do everything you reasonably can to prevent damage to your car, the cars of others and/or injury to yourself or others. That is just for street use of a car. On a track, the safety and preparation expectations and requirements of most sponsoring organizations is even higher, and the assumptions of the risk that you take for your actions, and those of others, is higher as well. Nobody is forcing you to drive on the track, and certainly you should not allow anybody to persuade you to do it. Thoroughly investigate and study first, and then make up your own mind.

Once you have made the decision that you are going to drive a car on a race track, then it is your responsibility to do it as safely and intelligently as you can, for your own sake and that of those around you. Such care includes your careful preparation of the car, its transport to and from the track, and staging in the garage and pits. It includes your personal skill development and preparation through driving schools and practice in car control on and off the track. It also includes how you enter the track, how you leave the track at the end of your session, how you evaluate the risk areas of the track and develop your plans to deal with those risks.

Be mentally, emotionally and physically prepared for the stresses. The level of concentration required is more intense and sustained than any driving experience you have had on the street, and possibly more than any other experience you have ever had anywhere. The faster you go, the more data you have to deal with, and the less time and distance to deal with it, and however good you think you are, or actually are, sooner or later you will find you are not good enough at some point, in some corner, on some day. That is not good or bad. It is just the way it is.

While you cannot eliminate all of the risks associated with high performance driving, you can do a lot to reduce and to manage risks by proper preparation of yourself and your car, attention to safety at all levels of equipment and driving techniques, and by running with reputable organizations and sponsors of track day events. Please do all of that and more.

The satisfaction that comes from driving a very fast lap derives from an assembly of many little things. It takes time, practice and study to get it right, and patience is a virtue. Fast driving does not come from deciding that you want to drive "fast" and stepping harder on the gas and brake pedals of a car with a big engine. Rather it comes from developing the car control and driving skills to accelerate, turn, brake, shift and balance weight on the car **smoothly and precisely** under a wide array of differing conditions and circumstances. As you improve those skills… speeds increase, lap times decrease, and more importantly your errors should decrease. Slow is *smooth*, and smooth becomes *fast*.

What defines **"fast" is what is fast for you.** Compared to a horse, you will be going very fast, and for a turtle… even more so. Yet for a beam of light or radio wave you will be virtually stationary! As to other drivers… don't get trapped into that element of competition. It is of no emotional importance that somebody else in a different car is a few seconds slower or faster than you.

If you want to be competitive against others in your driving, and there are many people who do, there are organizations that arrange competitions for "time attack" or racing against the clock versus other drivers, as well as the traditional and popular "wheel to wheel" racing. Those are not HPDE and should not be confused with HPDE. If you want to do that type of competitive driving, get yourself into a proper racing organization and follow their program.

In HPDE, there is no blood, honor or money on the table. No fashion beauties with bouquets of flowers, no gigantic bottles of champagne to spray adoring fans, no poster sized checks for amazing sums of money, await you for being the fastest driver on the track.

The goal is to learn to drive as skillfully as you can as safely as you can at speeds within the capabilities of yourself, the car, and the track under the specific conditions of the day, and then go home at day's end with car and body unscathed.

Know your limitations. Driving this course is terrific fun, but you must recognize and respect the limitations of the track, the car, and yourself with clarity. While most beginners approach track days with the reserve and caution appropriate to reduce risk of mishap, a lapse of attention in the slow Turn 17 is without mercy, and the Roval is intimidating to anyone with active brain function. There is perhaps a greater risk on this track for the intermediate and advanced drivers who are pushing the envelope of performance limits for their cars, and their own driving skills, but at higher speeds than they may be used to. Control recovery at high speed is more difficult, and the consequences of lost control to man and machine more severe, particularly with high speed drops before sharp, slow turns such as 3, 10 and 13, so respect this attribute of speed when driving Auto Club Speedway, where corners that are technically simple at slower speeds like the chicane of 7/8 and the double left of 14/15 develop subtle nuances at higher speeds that can surprise the driver.

The front "straight" is actually a long, eleven degree banked curve. Once you enter the straight, pick your driving line and stick to it.

Crossing start/finish line. Complete pass before end of straight, and prepare for smooth transition on corner entry to Turn 1.

Track Entry

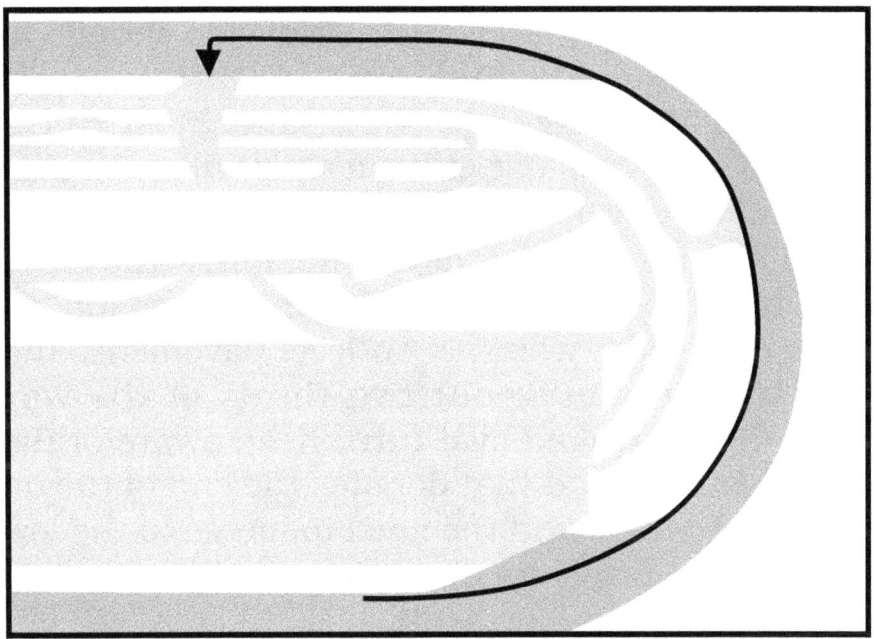

Safety for both the entering car and the cars on track is a priority for every road course and participant. Every track has a unique set of issues associated with its track entry and its track exit. You need to study and understand both track entry and exit procedure and technique *before* you show up. Given the high speeds of on track cars near the track entry point at Auto Club Speedway, and the blend line at the tight Turn 3, special attention must be paid to this aspect of driving the course.

Track entry is from the hot pit to the left of the main straight, just before the banked oval of Turns 1 and 2. Assembly at the grid for start is usually through the eastern most of the tunnels that go beneath the infield stands fronting the hot pits. Cars turn immediately left upon exiting the tunnel, before the hot pit lane, into a grid wide enough to allow three abreast configuration, and approximately fifteen cars per lane. Most HPDE session starts will use either a single file or double file grid arrangement, and perhaps 25 cars.

When released by the starter, follow the entry lane and stay below the wide painted lane line on your right side, which is on level pavement, and which continues about two thirds of the way around the banked oval turn. Keep aware of the grass patch ahead that denotes the end of the off track entry lane and the need to merge to the low line of the track itself, which at that point is approximately 50 feet wide.

Follow the left lane on to the track, and stay left within the painted white entry line as cars rounding the banked turn may be going 150 mph or faster as they come down the high bank exiting the Roval and track out towards the wall on the far right. Even though you may be going 80 mph or faster by this point, the potentially high variance in speed of 70 mph or more at the corner apex point for the on track car beside the entry lane is substantial, and the maneuvering options for the on track car are limited if the entering car slips in front of them. Check your mirrors for cars approaching from the right rear. Stay tight left along the track edge to the right to left corner of Turn 3 and thus out of the driving line of the cars on track, then dip left into Turn 3. This entry line will not be the ideal driving line for either Turn 3 or Turn 4, but you will be able to be WOT exiting Turn 4 and at full track speed by entry to Turn 5.

(**Beginner's note:** At the release by the starter you cannot see behind you far enough, either over your shoulder or with your mirrors, to accurately pick up cars already on track in the front straight, and which will be potentially upon you as you enter the track as they exit the Roval Turn 2. Accordingly, to be safe you must adhere to the track entry protocol that requires you to stay left all the way down the segment of the back straight that leads to Turn 3. As you circle around the bottom of the Roval check your mirrors for cars entering that corner behind you. As you are approaching Turn 3 you should be able to see cars approaching from behind and tracking out to the right, positioning to follow the optimal race driving line through Turns 3 and 4. Do not wander off the tight left edge driving line for entering cars, as you will be intruding into their maximum thresh hold braking zone or their corner entry turn in zone, nor should you suddenly adjust speed or do anything that is unpredictable.)

While it is the overtaking driver's responsibility to execute a safe pass, it is the entering driver's responsibility to assist in the exercise of good judgment of the overtaking driver to be correct in his "pass or follow" decision by being predictable. The overtaking driver will be coming down the exit of Turn 2 and able to see the entering car on the left, calculate the closure rate, and make a judgment on whether he can safely pass on the right and enter the turn first, or slow down enough to follow the entering car into Turn 3. Although the driving lines of the two cars will be different through Turn 3 and Turn 4, the relative speeds will be fairly close, and the closure rates slower, with the on track over taking car having the wider radius arc and thus higher speed of the two going into Turn 3.

THE ROVAL OF TURNS 1 AND 2

Turn 1 corner entry. Smoothly adjust speed to desired corner entry velocity, head up and vision to left into the corner.

Turn 1 with fourteen degree banking. Hold to driving line and steady to slight squeeze on throttle.

Turn 2 apex is low along white stripe. Lateral inertia will move car wide right towards wall. Grip lessens with grit and marbles close to wall, so keep it a fun day by not painting the wall and stay at least one car width away.

Turn 2 exit to right. Keep safe distance from wall on right.

The Roval of Turns 1 and 2

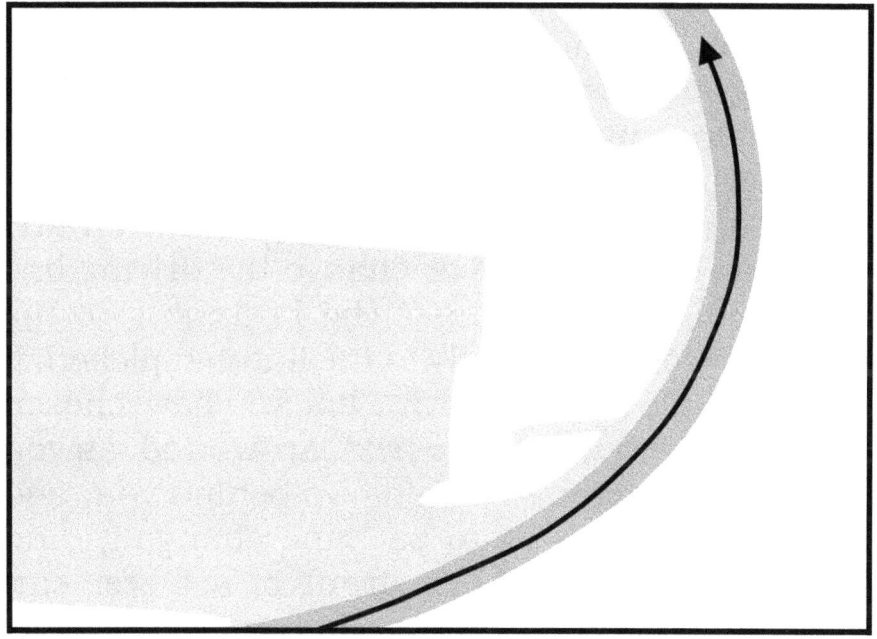

As you exit the infield portion of the auto competition course you merge into the lower section of the front straight of the NASCAR oval at the exit of that circuit's Turn 4. You should be able to up shift to fourth gear at or slightly before entering the front straight and gradually track out to the high speed line at about center track or perhaps one car width above. There is no advantage to going higher and closer to the wall, and indeed the accumulation of dust and "marbles" (those clumps of melted tire rubber that are sloughed off with higher wheel speeds and thrown upon the track and the cars behind) reduce the adhesion of your tires, so it is best to keep at least two car widths away from the wall. There is no drive through beverage service up there, so stay well away from it.

(**Beginner's note:** With 75 feet of track width on the big straight you may have some indecision about where to take your driving line. You can experiment from one lap to another, but on any given lap don't wobble or change the driving line once you set your line at the beginning of the straight. Hold steadfastly to the line you picked. If you conclude that the driving line you have chosen is not ideal, change it the next lap around, as you may have faster cars coming up behind you, and it can be dangerous to be "lane changing" and inadvertently slipping in front of a faster car. Predictability in your driving line is an especially important aspect of safety to all cars for this part of the course, which means all the way around the track to the entry to Turn 3).

As you smoothly drift up to your driving line and towards the wall, holding the accelerator to the floor, up shift at just before redline to fifth gear and then again around the start finish line to sixth gear, if you have it. It is a rare road course that puts any car into top gear and holding the accelerator down to the floor for any period of time, especially for large displacement and exotic V-8, V-10 and V-12 powerplants, with five and six speed gearboxes, but this track section is one of them. The top gear howl of Ferrari and Lamborghini, and the deep growl of Corvette and Viper engines, to name only these four, is at their finest through the start finish line and down to the entry to Turn 1.

You will notice from the track map that the "straight" is really the curved part of the letter "D", and this track is described as a D shaped oval. While not as dramatic a curve as the type face of that letter in this writing, you will definitely see and feel the track curvature as you literally scream down the eleven degree banked segment at what for most of you is the fastest speed, legal or otherwise, you ever have and perhaps ever will experience in a car. Hold the accelerator down and concentrate your vision far ahead into the Roval corner to set your entry line properly.

All that talk and reading you have experienced about taking the most efficient driving line suddenly becomes one of the more fascinating and importantly relevant parts of your personal knowledge base, as the concrete wall and barrier fence at the top of the track loom before you; indeed it almost feels as though the wall is coming to you rather than the other way around... and coming fast. (If you have not engaged in talk and reading about driving lines... you should not be on this track behind the wheel.) Most cars will be at their absolute maximum velocity, or very close to it, at this time. This will either be due to a speed governor programmed into the ECU, or the horsepower and torque of the car no longer being able to overcome the resistance of the air. The street car with ratings of over 300 bhp will be at or over 150 mph, and boosted (supercharger/ turbocharger) versions with a reprogrammed ECU chip, or the exotic super cars with 500 bhp can be at 175 mph or higher as the entry to Turn 1 presents itself.

Aerodynamic stability is a major consideration and inputs to steering and braking, even lifting throttle, are of critical import relative to the same inputs at 50 mph lower speeds, and control can be a matter of thin margins. Suspension capability and tire grip is also critical, as the springs will compress more at high speed against the banked surface in the corner, and lateral inertial force will be pushing you towards the wall on the high side. Be steady, be smooth, be firm, but be gentle, and above all be "aware" of what the car is doing and why it is doing it, so you do not feed an incorrect input into the dynamics with either your hands or your feet. If you feel the need to hiccup, belch, whimper or otherwise squirm, stretch, twitch or scratch, get it over with prior to turn in. Once you commit to the corner at the limits, there are few options for significant alteration to your plan of attack. You should not be hearing your tires squeal in this corner, and if you do, take it slower.

(**Beginner's note:** The operative concern here is "the limits" of you and your car. Stay well below them and this corner is just a cool slingshot run and comparatively safe. Do not fall prey to the arrogant assumption that the outstanding engineering of your car is matched by your driving prowess. Especially if you are in a high performance car.)

As you begin your set up to corner entry for the Roval, mark your velocity, your turn in point, and smoothly slough speed to what you want for corner entry velocity. At high speed a braking for entry to this corner usually is not necessary, as the sheer resistance of the air will act like a brake when you lift throttle. But if you do feel the need to brake, or lift throttle, do it smoothly and gradually, don't stab the brake or lift throttle totally or abruptly. Otherwise you will find the nose of the car pushing down as if from a giant invisible hand from the aerodynamic force, and the rear lifting up as you begin turning, and that forward weight transfer is conducive to losing rear wheel traction and sliding the rear of the car. Instead, you want to reduce speed gradually (it will not take long with the air resistance at that velocity!) and then ease once more into the throttle to settle the rear of the car as you turn into the first corner.

Mark the driving line (you can make it anywhere you are comfortable getting around, but initially consider keeping it at not more than 1 and a half car widths above the center line), and keep your eyes up looking through the corner. (That means slightly to the left of the left headlamp position). Otherwise if you look down the nose of the car at the track surface, and then raise your head square and straight, you will be looking right at the wall and it can promote a moment of indecision, hesitation, or hypnosis, leading you in just an instant to drive up the bank towards the wall, and perhaps over input right to left steering in response, putting greater demands on the adhesion of the tires. Sliding butt first into the wall is not and should not be part of anyone's plan for the day, so understanding what leads to it helps you to understand what you need to NOT do, which can be just as important as understanding what you SHOULD do.

Hold the steering input steady on the driving line, keep the throttle steady, keep your head and eyes up throughout, and mark the exit apex point low on the left. Unless you start to under steer or "push" the front tires through the turning input, do not lift off your maintenance throttle, indeed if anything be breathing on just a touch more. The sensation of speed, lateral push to the outside wall, roar of the engine reverberating off the wall and back into the passenger side open window, g-force pressure and compression of the suspension

THE ROVAL OF TURNS 1 AND 2

against the banking is unique, like nothing else you have ever experienced on a sustained basis at most other track layouts. Stay steady, keep your breathing controlled against the g-force and do not become fixated on the wall. Smoothly maintain your driving line and sweep down off the banking low and into the apex point, and be squeezing back on to full throttle as you roar down the high banking into the back straight.

The track out lateral inertial momentum of the corner pushes you towards the concrete wall on the right. You may be going about 135 to 140 mph at this point, and in a boosted car 165 mph or more (the acceleration coupled with a bit of gravity assist coming down off the banking gives the car a noticeable "goose" even with the high speed resistance of the air.) Don't fight the drift momentum taking you to the wall, but don't get closer than three to five feet either. (Beginners, stay at least two car widths away.) There is a hard braking segment before Turn 3 requiring you to shed 80 to 110 mph before the infield section, and you don't want to waggle your nose or tail into the wall, a risk that is increased by the "marbles" and grit we talked about earlier.

(**Beginner's note:** Take this section with an instructor several times, indeed as many times as you need. If possible, take it riding in the passenger seat with an instructor driving a few times as well, before you go solo. This is no place to feel embarrassed about going slower than you think others may be going. The "pucker factor" of the Roval is unique, and while we don't need to debate whether it is surpassed by other track challenges around the world, it certainly ranks high up the scale. So respect it and yourself, and understand both it and yourself well, before you challenge it.)

As you gain more experience with this corner it will become one of your absolute favorite experiences in track running. There are certain corners that require great respect and appreciation for what is going on, and which have a tendency to collect the high intermediate to advanced driver whose concentration or respect wanes ever so slightly, or whose skill sets are not developed sufficiently to recover car control instantly. Turn 9 at Willow Springs, Turn 6 at Laguna Seca, Turn 10 at Sears Point, the Bus Stop at Buttonwillow and the Kink at Road America are among this category of hard consequences for a high speed mistake type turns, and the Roval at California Speedway deserves a place among them.

Turn 3 entry is very late and wide.

Turn 3 apex is late and aligns car to left side of track.

Turn 3 exit is transition to entry to Turn 4. Maximization of Turn 4 corner exit speed is priority.

Turn 4 apex is late to increase radius arc.

Turns 3 and 4

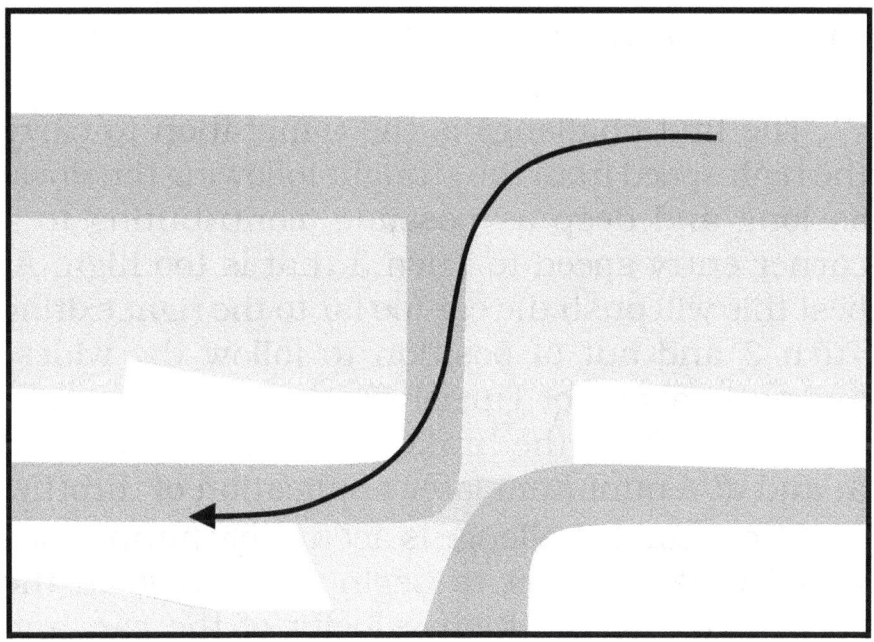

This section now takes the driver on a back and forth twisty romp through the infield of the NASCAR oval. But don't despair at the thought that this means slow speeds and gimmicky tight turns like a miniature golf layout. The infield is 130.7 acres, more than enough space for a championship 18 hole golf course, and there are two straight runs where many cars will be well over 100 mph!

Turns 3 and 4 are a compound pair of linked left-right 90 degree corners leading to a medium-short straight. Therefore, maximum corner exit speed from Turn 4 has priority over maximum velocity into and through Turn 3. Sacrificing maximum corner speed in Turn 3 to set up Turn 4 is conceptually simple as a conclusion, but smooth execution is quite challenging for two reasons.

The first challenge is the temptation to carry the high speed from the straight following the Roval as long and deep as possible, contributing to a corner entry speed to Turn 3 that is too high. At best this will push the car too far to the right exiting Turn 3 and out of position to follow the widest and optimal arc for Turn 4. That may then require another stab on the brakes between Turn 3 and 4, and at a minimum later application of throttle.

The second challenge is accurately hitting your initial braking point to begin the attack on the corner, due to the high velocity of the car, and efficiently applying the sustained maximum threshold braking to drop between 80 and 110 mph, the three or even four gear downshifts during the braking run, and hitting the turn in point precisely when you have reached the velocity you want as you squirt through the stacks of tires on the left and right sides of the entry and exit to Turn 3.

Note that precise rev matching during downshifting is important, as you will cause a disconcerting jerk to the car on re-engagement of the transmission if you have not raised the rpm level sufficiently. Apart from being hard or potentially damaging to the transmission, it will also upset the balance of the car. (Did anyone mention the concrete wall just a couple of feet off to the right side of the car while all this is going on?)

If you do not have the heel/toe rev matching downshift technique yet, this is a corner that conclusively demonstrates the benefits from that technique. Trying to brake, then lift from the brake pedal with your right foot to blip the throttle and downshift and then move the right foot back to re-brake, and repeat the cycle two or three times, will unsettle the balance of the car, pitching it forward and backward and also greatly extend the braking zone you require to slow the car because you are off the brakes to shift multiple times, as contrasted to having steady constant pressure all through your shorter braking zone. An option can be to apply sustained braking and wait until you are slowed to just before corner entry and make one direct downshift from sixth gear to third or second gear, with proper attention to grabbing second or third and not first or fourth gear by mistake! But you still have the final down shift where you have to get off the brake, and that is a serious disadvantage compared to someone who has perfected the heel/toe technique.

Set this corner entry from the far right edge of the wide back straight (with a safe distance between you and the wall), plan for a very late entry and apex point to Turn 3 to allow entry to Turn 4 from the left side of the short section linking Turn 3 to Turn 4. As you complete your braking and begin turn in to Turn 3 you will be squeezing back on throttle smoothly to begin accelerating through the corner and the transition from the left edge entry to Turn 4. The objective is to be at or close to wide open throttle at the apex of Turn 4 simultaneously with having the tires close to the limits of adhesion through the widest possible radius arc in the mid corner section of Turn 4.

   If you have more power than the tires can handle while turning you will of course need to back off the throttle to keep the tires gripping. The car will track out to the left side of the surface, then proceed to up shift to third or possibly fourth gear and immediately apply a touch of steering to glide smoothly back to the right edge, and set up for the right to left horseshoe hairpin corner of Turns 5 and 6.

   The demands on your braking equipment are intense here, and also before the compound Turns 9 and 10, and again at Turns 13 and 14, so you should be alert to the possibility of brake fade. For intermediate and advanced drivers, be aware that a heavy street car can overtax your braking system in just a few laps on this circuit. You may need to upgrade to a larger rotor and caliper brake kit, install braided stainless brake lines and use a top rated racing brake fluid and more aggressive bite brake pads if you are going to run hard for ten consecutive laps during a session.

(**Beginner's note:** Negotiating this corner, indeed all corners, should focus on safety and smoothness before speed. A lot is happening for this corner that happens in every corner, there is just "more" of it. More speed, more braking, more gear downshifting. Give yourself the room and time you need to manage this corner smoothly, concentrating on keeping the balance of the car stable. Just apply the brakes a little earlier. A two tenths of a second delay in starting your braking run can put you fifty feet farther down the track and hopelessly out of position to make the turn. If that happens, just keep the wheel straight, run through the line of rubber cones and into the back straight and slow down, turn about and creep back towards the corner station, where the corner worker will wave you back on to the track and into the turn when it is safe to do so.

Run between the cones, not over them, for while they may bend and crumple, they also tend to wedge or jam between the car body and the ground and drag with you, and if they are touching any part of your exhaust or other hot parts, they melt, creating a mess, smoke, stink etc.

You will have a head on view of the approaching cars as you return to the track, so be sure that in addition to waiting for the corner worker to direct you back on to the track, that you confirm it is safe to re-enter. Steady brake pressure while downshifting three or four times in a straight line and arriving at your corner entry turn in point at the desired speed, with a generous margin for safety, is a good initial challenge, together with picking a precise initial braking and turn in point.)

Turn 4 exit is on left edge. Immediately transition back to right edge of surface.

TURNS 5 AND 6

Turn 5 corner entry for single apex approach is from wide right and late.

Turn 6 corner apex is late. Camber is flat and throttle on oversteer common here.

Turn 6 exit has extra paving on right and you can use it.

Turns 5 and 6

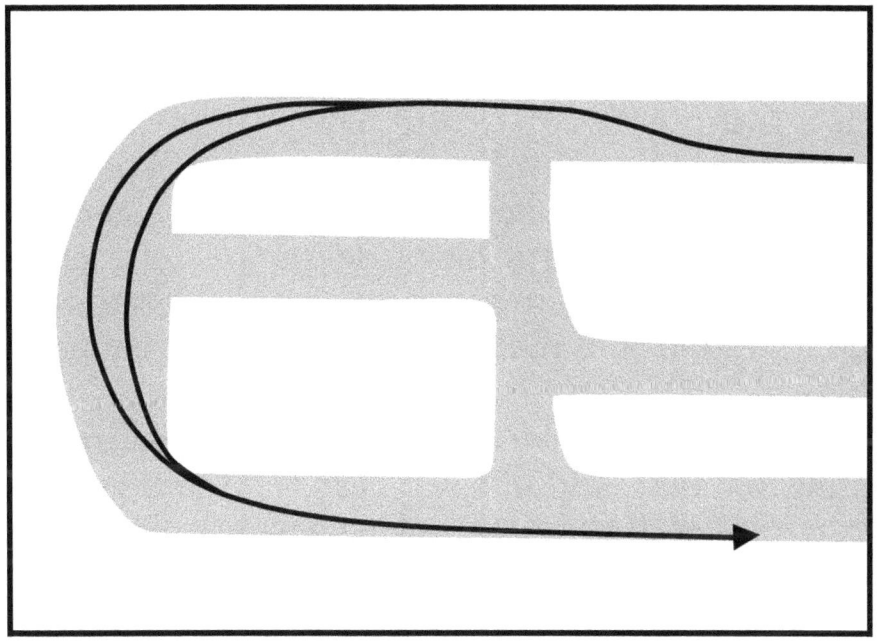

This hairpin presents a widened 180 degree corner (two ninety degree corners with a very short straight connection of a few yards) that can be taken either as a double apex corner, or as a very late single apex corner, with some extra paved track out room on the right edge at corner exit for both techniques to exploit.

For the *single apex approach*, straight brake before corner entry, downshift, and look over your left shoulder to spot your exit apex. Keep your focus on the corner apex and bring the front of the car around, squeezing throttle and feeling and listening to the tire adhesion all the way through the corner. This is an excellent corner to learn the language of how the tires "talk" to you about what they are doing and how much adhesion they have left to give you.

The camber is flat, so be careful that you do not induce throttle on over steer in your exuberance to get as much corner exit speed as possible. There is some room to counter steer and catch a slide, and a bit of deliberate rotation is fine, but you need to be ready with quick hands to do it, and loss of rear wheel adhesion is common here.

On exit hug the right side of the track and up shift to fourth and in some cars then fifth gear as you proceed easterly towards the high speed chicane of Turns 7 and 8.

For the *double apex approach*, from the right edge turn in slightly to mark an approach to the corner entry or first apex, straight brake hard, with your initial braking point being later than for the single apex approach, downshift to third and possibly second gear, and look over your left shoulder to spot your exit apex, which will be slightly earlier than the single apex approach due to your lower speed.

Keep your focus on the exit apex point and bring the front of the car around, squeezing throttle and feeling the adhesion. This approach definitely can benefit from deliberately induced oversteer to rotate the rear of the car, and with lower speed and more room for error is relatively safe to try, with the same caveats as noted above.

Which of the two approaches is best will really depend on your car's handling characteristics and your driving skills. You will need to try both of them out to work out whether either of these, or a compromise between the two, delivers the best lap time.

(Beginner's note: This corner has a lot of run off room and a relatively slower speed, so you can work a bit more aggressively here at learning the limits of your tires and counter steering to catch rear rotation from over steer, or experiencing under steer and how to breathe (not lift) throttle and straighten steering a bit to regain front traction.

You may also experience "lift throttle" over steer in this turn by too rapidly lifting off the gas and with the combination of weight transfer pitching forward and the lateral g forces of the corner... exchange in a very short instant the experience of under steer for over steer. This is a good corner that can teach you a lot about commanding a car through it without too many serious consequences if you lose control, as long as you are not in close proximity to other cars, and you immediately put "both feet in" (clutch and brake pedals to the floor) should you spin.

Remember to keep your head up and looking through the corner exit of Turn 6 to identify the possibility of a car losing control in front of you, as well as watching the corner worker to the right edge of the track on corner entry to Turn 5 for an indication if something has gone awry out of your field of vision to the left.)

Note heavy loading on right rear in mid-corner transition between Turns 5-6.

Prepare for the Unexpected

A few words about safely getting by a suddenly distressed car in front of you. This section of track at Auto Club Speedway presents a good spot to remind ourselves that all of us are out on a track to have a good time as safely as possible. But sometimes events will unfold that are not on the menu of "good time", and you need to be prepared to deal with them.

Most of the occasions on track when a car gets into difficulty that presents a potential or actual risk to others, the corner workers at their flag stations and connected by their radio sets to each other will be signaling track conditions in front of you that allow you to take appropriate and safe measures to manage the hazard. Know the flags!

Most events involving an off track excursion or other hazard transpire from start to finish in a matter of only a few seconds, and somewhere other than right in front of you. With typical track lengths of 2.5 to 3.5 miles and lap times of between 1:45

and 3:00 minutes, you often have an abundance of time and space to be warned and prepared. By the time you arrive at the scene, the car involved may already be back on track and on its way such that you never even see it before it reaches the track exit. Or the last wisps of dust and tire smoke are wafting away and the car is stationary.

But eventually, and it could be your first day out or your fiftieth, somebody is going to "lose it" in front of you in close enough proximity that advance corner worker flag signals are not relevant.

You are on your own judgment and skill to avoid disaster, and it is on you immediately.

It could be a loss of control by the driver of that car. It could be the surprise of a part falling off such as a lug nut, exhaust pipe, body panel, even a drive shaft, or a fluid being discharged from a blown coolant hose or engine oil. It could be a small animal bolting across the track, or a plastic bag blowing on to your windshield. It could be you losing your brakes, or having other control problems too. Your engine may quit, clutch pedal stick to the floor, or steering fail. All things mechanical can break, and many of them do break. I have lost a piston rod under boost going through the Roval, and brakes going into Turn 13 at Auto Club Speedway, been close behind a car that spun into Turn 14, and another that nosed into the tire wall at Turn 17. All without any real risk of harm or mishap to myself or others. It is part of the experience.

Desert tortoises are known to have crossed the track at Spring Mountain in Pahrump, and armadillos, deer, dogs, possum, raccoon, coyote, squirrel, jack rabbit, and other creatures are not uncommon jaywalkers on many circuits elsewhere. I took a bumblebee off the face shield going down the front straight of Auto Club Speedway one day, which was quite the juicy mess across the headliner of the car. Wet leaves, pine needles, dust and grit, rubber marbles, not to mention oil, water, coolant, brake fluid, steering fluid... the possibilities of surprise challenge are without limit. You don't get to choose, you must be ready for anything. Every lap is new and different and you must be focused in your concentration without lapses.

If you are following another car, even at a distance of 20 or 30 car lengths, you should have them in your vision clearly as your head should be up. This hairpin corner of Turns 5 and 6 at California Speedway reflects a classic corner where as you are preparing for your turn in for corner entry, you should be monitoring the car in front and aware of whether it has negotiated the track out on the right edge successfully. If that car in front has dropped one or more wheels off the right edge, or is spinning or waggling from loss of traction, you have time to back off the throttle and give room and time for the events in front of you to unfold, including if necessary to slow down or stop or even deliberately leave the track surface should that be the safest alternative left available to you.

You should not assume that because the car in front of you has drifted off to the right that it is safe to pass on the left or that the other driver is even aware of your presence. Indeed it should be presumed that the driver ahead has his/her hands very full with the challenge of car control and has lost all focus on everything else.

One risk is that they could compound their track out error of running off the right edge with an overcorrection that launches them across the track from right to left, hammering the throttle and taking a path to the left could simply cause one of you to go nose first into the side of the other in a violent collision.

As the overtaking car it is your responsibility to manage a pass safely.

You have the advantage of being in control of your car and seeing everything in front of you, while the car in front of you does not. Accordingly, with your priority being safety, and not the achievement of your personal best lap time on this lap, *slow down*. This does not mean that you should slam on your brakes and create a second potential hazard to cars approaching from behind, and a compounding of the danger and complexity of safe passage. Rather, with the knowledge of who is behind you and how close from having checked your mirrors on the straight approach to the Turn 5-6 hairpin, you begin your safe evasion of the problem in front.

If the driver in front exhibits a controlled exit and slowing off track to the right, safely pull off line to the left and pass, then merge back on to the driving line to the right edge and set up for the Chicane of Turns 7 and 8.

If the driver in front is spinning on the track surface, apply brake smoothly and slow down while carefully watching the direction of his momentum and what the car is doing. If he/she is "both feet in" (clutch and brake pedals fully depressed) and sliding to the left edge, stay oriented right and manage your speed to be able to take safe evasive action if there is a sudden and unexpected change in the direction or dynamic of the car in front, such as a roll or flip or sudden regaining of traction, so that you can stop without colliding.

You want to get safely by the event if you can, so that approaching cars from behind are not an additional danger to you or the car in trouble. Once you are past the event and out of immediate danger yourself, you can follow the directions of the corner workers, which may be a simple yellow flag caution, or a black flag to all drivers to come in to the pits under caution, or even a red flag to all drivers to come to a full and complete on course stop until directed to restart.

What a lot of your study to driving a course efficiently does is highlight the places where not only you might get into trouble, but where other drivers are likely to get into trouble and how and why. You should analyze what you ought to do as a driver should that trouble occur to you, so that you have prepared for it and can react quickly... there is no time for leisurely reflection in the midst of the challenge. You should know where the run off areas are, where the walls or other obstacles are. You should have already determined what you need to be doing and why and how before you ever get there. You should also have maintained sufficient track awareness that you know whether there are cars approaching from behind so that your recovery efforts are going to be among the safer options.

That preparation for what you are going to do if you get in trouble also helps you to understand what the likely dynamics of a car in front of you are going to be should it be in distress, and what is likely to transpire as the driver struggles for control, so you can act accordingly as the following car to avoid further mishap to either of you.

This should be a part of your preparation and study for driving every corner on every course before you strap in to your car to drive it. And then closely note in your orientation laps with your instructors, and in your own warm up laps, the action options and whether they match up to your expectations from your track map reviews, in car videos you have watched and discussions with other drivers. If the sponsor organization offers an orientation ride around the track for drivers, by all means do it. Even better, try to get the opportunity to walk or bicycle around the track.

A slow, close up look at the track will reveal subtle undulations, changes in camber, surface grip conditions, run off area characteristics and much more. If you can do it with four or five other drivers, you will pick up much valuable information during your conversation as you journey around the circuit.

If you creep left you will increase the severity of the lateral load shift from left to right for entry to Turn 8, and thus the transfer from right to left through and exiting Turn 8. This significantly increases chance of leaving track surface on left at corner exit from Turn 8.

Align driving path to minimize weight shift between corners. On throttle from corner entry.

Stay on throttle through corner exit.

Turns 7 and 8

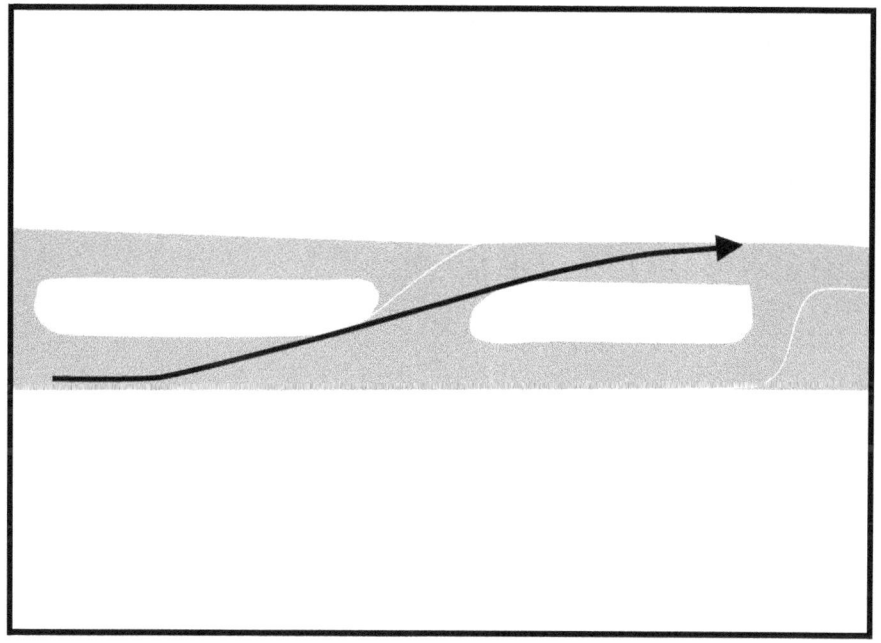

The Chicane is an exercise in transitioning inertial load or "weight" from left to right and back to left as smoothly yet briskly as you can while maintaining maximum velocity through the corner. You have a reasonable amount of room on corner exit from Turn 8 to collect your balance, so the key is to be patient and wait on your turn in to

Turn 7, and resist the temptation to "crab" early into the corner entry. Done properly you can maintain throttle, or just lift a little before turn entry and then ease back on to keep the rear settled, and "thread the needle" through this corner at over 100 mph, by "straightening" the segment from the apex of Turn 7 to the apex of Turn 8.

(Beginner's note: Concentrate on learning to induce the transfer of weight from side to side gently, not on going as fast as you can. You want to be able to make the car "take a set" predictably before you start increasing velocity here, or else you can find yourself going off track to the left on exit from Turn 8 at high speed.)

Turn 9

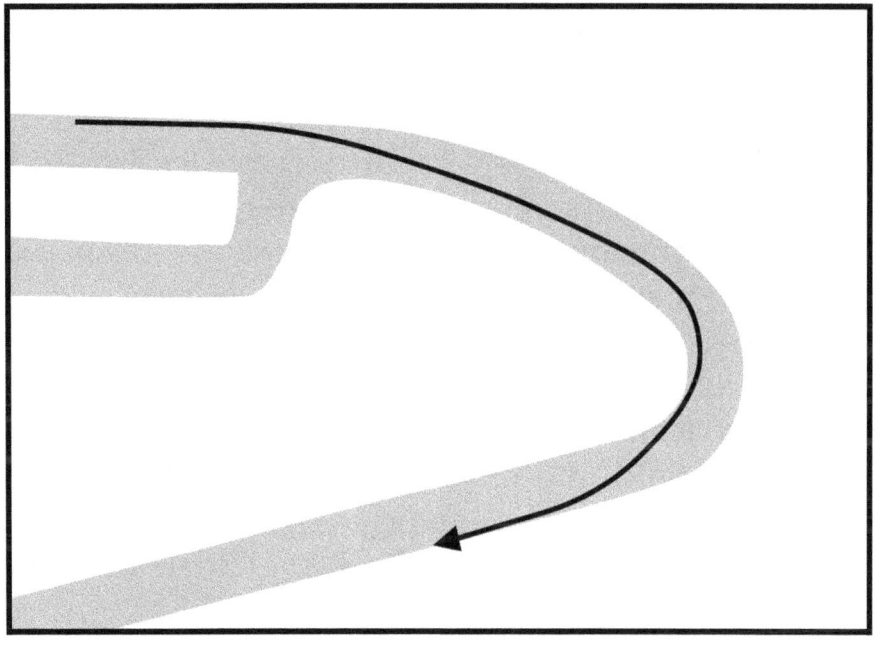

As you thread through the chicane, the track transitions into the gradually diminishing radius arc of Turn 9, whose primary purpose is to provide a segment to settle the car after the chicane, provide a braking zone and set up for the sharp button hook corner of turn 10, which then leads to a long infield straight section. Therefore you want to *maintain* velocity out of Turn 8, tracking out to the left edge of the pavement, then turn slightly to the right to make a straight run through the "corner" of Turn 9 to your turn in point for Turn 10, basically taking much of the corner curve out of Turn 9. Accelerate further into Turn 9 as you exit Turn 8, but not following the curvature of the left edge of the track surface, and then downshift from fourth or fifth gear to second gear under hard straight line braking to use all of the available grip of the tires for slowing (not turning *and* braking) to the slowest corner on the course. Because the corner is a gradual curve leading to a very slow and sharp hairpin corner, you must be mindful of the instability perils of downshifting and braking while asking your tires to manage any kind of lateral grip challenge from turning. This approach, to be far left on the surface, make an initial turn in and straighten steering to a target point for making a second turn in to the button hook hairpin of Turn 10, and then brake and down shift in a straight line to the target turn in point for your corner entry, takes much potential confusion out of the equation, gets you to the corner entry to Turn 10 faster, and allows later braking for corner entry. You may have a way that you prefer that is different and works better for you and for your car, but if you have not driven the course before, try a straighter driving line to reduce the possibility of losing the rear of the car in a right to left spin until you get familiar with the corner.

(**Beginner's note:** This is a deceptive corner due to its shape, and you can easily find yourself running out of track surface, braking force, foot speed/coordination for gear changes and directional options, all at the same time. Approach this corner slowly at first until you become settled into the optimal driving line.)

It is easy to get "lost" in this segment. Pick a reference point for your target, such as a light pole or fence support to mark your straight line from corner exit of Turn 8.

Taking the "straight line" path through Turn 9 allows driver to straight brake, then make corner entry turn in. You may wish to leave a little extra room on left if you want to rotate rear with oversteer into this slow speed corner.

Turn 10 corner apex is very late.

Turn 10

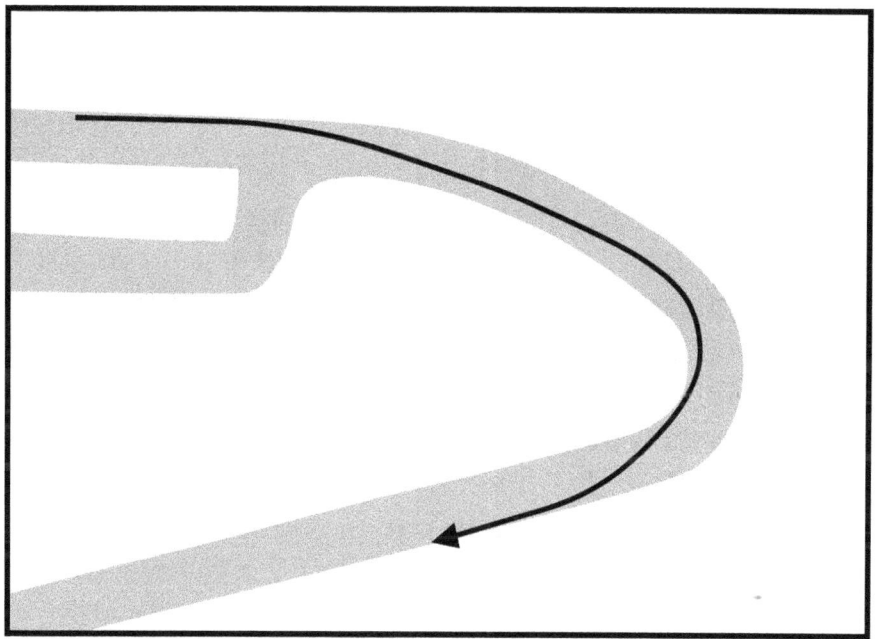

This corner is slow, but leads to a medium short straight, through a challenging acceleration chicane of Turns 11 and 12, and then continues to a medium infield straight. Therefore, a fast corner exit from Turn 10 carries benefits far down the infield and is to be prioritized.

A bit of trail braking at the end of Turn 9/ entry to Turn 10 can rotate the rear of the car and get the nose of the car pointed across the corner apex just a bit earlier and help you be on throttle sooner. You can also help that rotation with a little steering flick from left to right, and then catch it with counter steer if you are comfortable with that technique. If you are not experienced or comfortable with that technique, *don't try it here.* Instead, after a day of running Auto Club Speedway you may want to get some skid pad time and visualize the corner and play with the technique to get comfortable with the car's response to that combination of inputs, before you try it on the track. Rotation can be a way to set up a car for a faster exit speed in some, but most definitely not all, slow corners. You must balance the advantage of having an orientation of the car that will allow more power earlier for acceleration and less for turning, with the loss in speed from the initial rotation. As long as the car is sliding, it has lost grip to the track surface and thus power is not being applied to move the car forward. It should not be used in fast corners.

As you track out on corner exit to the left edge of the pavement, you will up shift to third and then fourth gear, and prepare to engage the combination of Turns 11 and 12.

(Beginner's note: This corner easily lures a driver into a much too early apex, which will take you off the surface on the left side, albeit at very low speed, unless you slow even more. The key here is to wait on the turn in until very late, and increase the geometry of the radius of the corner exit to as wide an arc as possible so you can apply more throttle and earlier, to get that corner exit speed higher.

The other "mind trick" of this corner is that it can seduce you into setting your corner entry turn in point too far to the right and too late into the corner. You must deliberately pick your corner entry target farther to the left, and earlier so that you do not go too deep. Again, draw the geometric path of the corner you want your car to describe to deliver the maximum corner exit speed and you may be surprised at what you find. An instructor ride along after you have driven a couple of sessions solo, to focus on this corner, can be time well spent.)

Corner exit to left edge and hold on edge until entry to Turn 11.

Turn 11 corner entry is from left edge of track surface at full throttle.

Turn 11 corner exit should align directly into corner apex of Turn 12. Track out space from Turn 12 is generous, so use all of it to keep accelerating rather than turning too abruptly into Turn 12 and either scrubbing speed or lifting throttle.

Turns 11 and 12

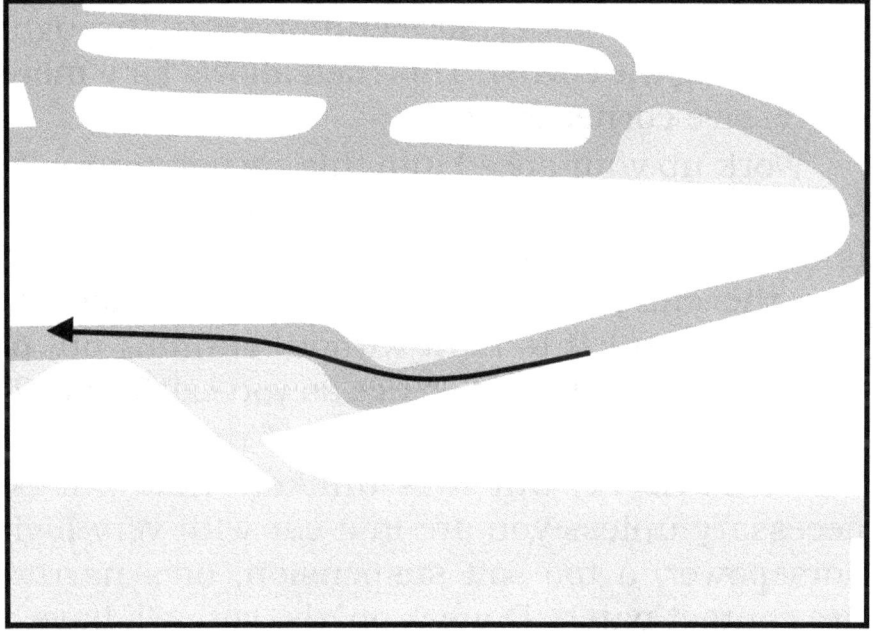

The ideal of taking this compound corner is to be WOT in third or fourth gear. The reality is that in many cars it is very hard to keep the pedal down to the floor at corner entry to Turn 11 as the turn in can be abrupt (and as it is often described by cones it can vary from event to event). If you cannot keep the adhesion you will clip the cones across the apex of Turn 12 on your left.

Avoiding early turn in on the corner entry to Turn 11 is the challenge... you must "wait" on the turn in to get a clear space through the gap. You have to transfer the weight to the left side smoothly, but also make the transition of weight quickly. There is plenty of track-out space on the right side after Turn 12 corner exit, so plan to use that space for a wide arc under acceleration into, through, and exiting the corner. This then allows for a more aggressive corner entry.

Work up your speed into this corner gradually so that you can feel the adhesion of the tires and find out how much speed you can manage to throw into the entry to Turn 11, and then smoothly transfer from left to right without running out of track surface on the right edge as you exit Turn 12.

If necessary, you can "breathe" throttle lightly before Turn 11, but it is unlikely that will be necessary unless you are in a car with very high horsepower, a too soft suspension, or a narrow tire contact patch. Done properly, you will have a full running acceleration from the very exit of Turn 10 all the way down the infield to the start of your braking run before entry to Turn 13.

Be aware that the corner is defined for most driving days by the placement of cones, and that can vary the challenge by tightening or loosening the geometry of the available corner radius. Keep that in mind as you review the course condition and layout on the first warm up lap so that you don't enter it too fast based on your last track day experience here.

Remember, the apex points are also marked with cones on many events, and that means that from event to event they can be different, and different enough to change your driving line materially and thus your technique of approach to the corners. So note them as being useful, but don't necessarily rely on them. Pick your own points and landmarks, preferably ones that cannot be moved or influenced by the opinions of others which may be incorrect.

(**Beginner's note:** This corner, like many, will not seem too difficult at first because you are not likely to be going fast enough at corner entry to test the limits of adhesion to your tires and suspension, unless you enter and apex the corner too early. Work on the inertial loading or weight balance transfer element, and as your corner exit speed from Turn 10 improves, you will find this corner holds increasing challenge to holding the ideal driving line and the reward for achieving it.)

Turn 12 track out to right edge. Note the "scrub" marks from tires to the right.

Turn 12 transition from right edge back to left edge, still under full throttle down infield straight.

Turn Segments 13, 14 and 15, 16

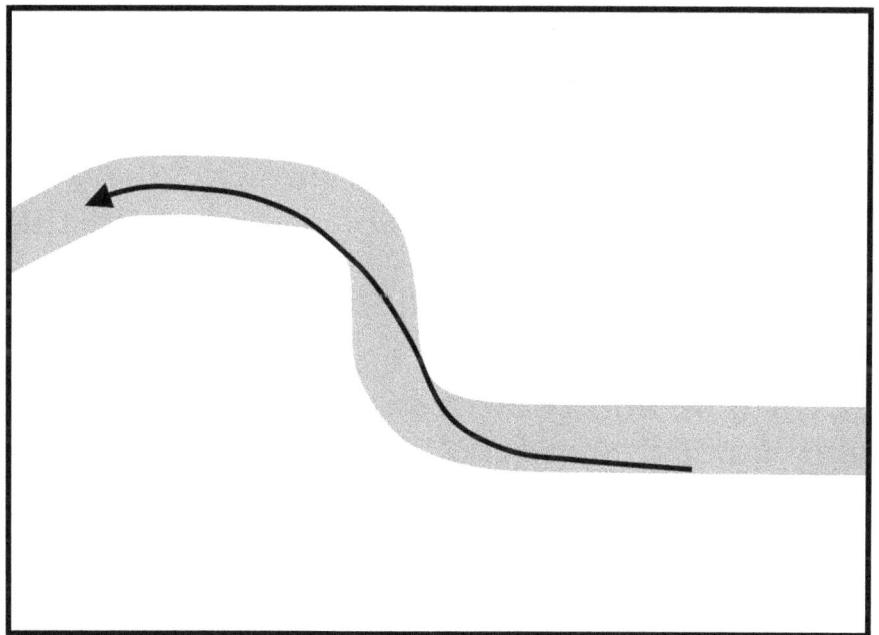

As you finish your track out from Turn 12, smoothly work your way across to the left edge of the track surface, up shift to fifth gear, and prepare for a very hard straight braking run from over 120 mph before entry to a "double" compound corner series, starting with a 90 degree left to right corner, which is complicated by the next corner that is right to left and about 90 degrees and slightly off camber, connecting immediately to another right to left corner of about 40 degrees, that itself immediately blends into a larger radius left to right corner of about 40 degrees.

This is not a series of corners that is going to gain the driver a lot of time, as much as it can and often does cost a lot of time.

A slower entry to Turn 13, followed by a smooth acceleration into and out of Turn 14, increasing gradually through the wider curvature of Turn 15, and then transferring weight from right to left under continuing acceleration through Turn 16 is the objective. There is a lot of finesse to this segment.

If you hammer the throttle too aggressively you will break traction through here easily. The corners of Turns 13 and 14 are marked with raised curbs, and handled imprudently you can be bouncing over them most unceremoniously, ruining your chance to slip through this section efficiently, and possibly mangling important pieces that are attached to your under carriage. While controlled brute force just moments before in Turns 11 and 12 may characterize that segment, this one is a more refined and delicate tip toe or dance, still at the limits, but all for the purpose of setting up the segment commencing with Turn 17 that precedes the long front straight.

TURN SEGMENTS 13, 14 AND 15, 16

Stay on the left edge of the pavement as you approach Turn 13, straight brake and drop two gears in most cars. Be very careful not to early apex your first turn in or it will ruin the entire segment. Smooth the weight transfer from side to side to help the car take a "set" and grip, especially in Turn 14 and as you smoothly accelerate and hold steering input into and through Turn 15. Be careful not to go too hard on throttle and break rear traction here, then up shift and transition back to a left to right corner while still holding and squeezing on the throttle through Turn 16, with your objective to come across the very right edge of the track surface at corner exit (rather than being over to the classic left side on track out of a left to right corner and out of position in this segment) for a short straight brake and downshift, leading to a sharp 110 degree right to left corner at Turn 17.

(**Beginners note:** Here you want to manage your car at the limits at moderate speed. There is a concrete wall on exit from Turn 14, so don't get frisky early in that corner as you transition to Turn 15. The most common mistake here is to enter Turn 13 with too much speed, putting the car on the extreme left of the track surface at entry to Turn 14, and thus ruining the next two or three corners. Slow down, take a very late apex into Turn 13, and then attack Turns 14 and 15 as a single element.)

Turn 13 entry should be late,

Stay to the right side to open up arc through Turn 14. Lead car is out of position and has blocked itself from optimal entry to Turn 14 from rushing entry to Turn 13.

On throttle through corner apex of Turn 14.

Transition to Turn 16 to stay on right edge of surface.

Entry to Turn 16 positions car on right edge.

Entry to Turn 17 from right edge.

Turn 17

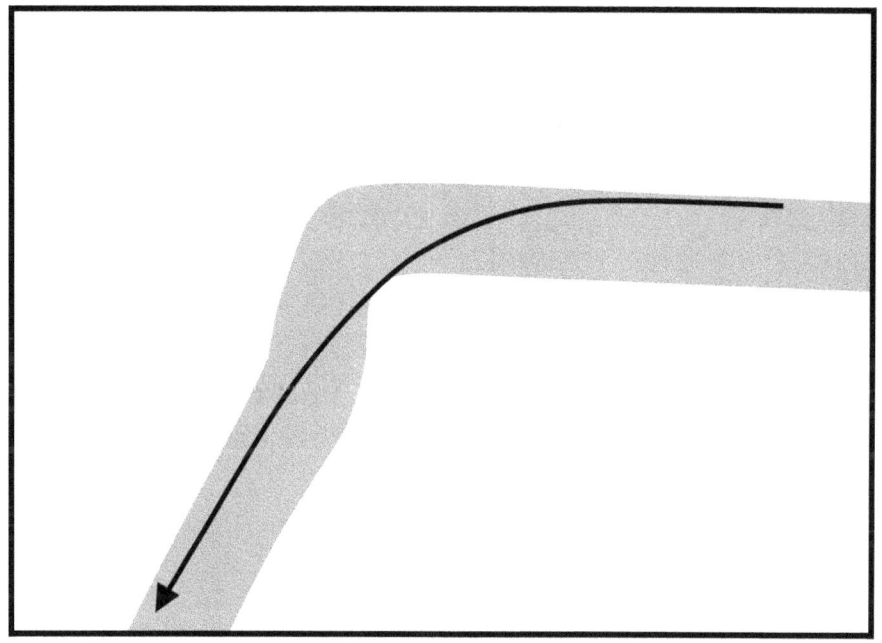

This is not a particularly daunting corner, except for the stacks and stacks of tires making up a wall on the right side and immediately behind. It is a narrow squeeze with absolutely no run off area and as a slow speed corner is not a place to be heroic, or stupid. Safety and strategy both compel a slower corner entry and faster corner exit, because the segment it leads to is almost all acceleration for fast entry to the front straight. You must be on the far right edge of the track surface on corner entry if you are to have any chance of getting around this corner quickly. Incorrect management of your driving line out of Turn 16 will ruin entry to Turn 17, and thus has a significant influence on lap time and speed that is carried all the way around to the entry to Turn 3. Accordingly, focus on being in the proper corner entry position for Turn 17, and under no circumstance make an early apex in Turn 17.

(Beginner's note: If you early apex or force too much speed into the corner, you can go nose first into the tire wall. With so little reward for aggressive driving, and so much risk, this turn is not to be taken lightly. Tire walls are very unfriendly to car body panels and drivers. Do not try to make a fast pass through here, just slow down and slip through it safely.)

TURN 17

Late turn in sets up late apex and avoids tire wall on right.

Stay right and prepare for sweeping entry to main straight.

This section to the main straight can get confusing. Work on developing a smooth "sweep" through this section as a single segment, rather than separate corner "pieces".

Grip limits are tested by continuing acceleration and cornering simultaneously. The driving line should follow as wide an increasing radius arc as available if you are at risk of breaking loose.

After Turn 17 to the Front Straight

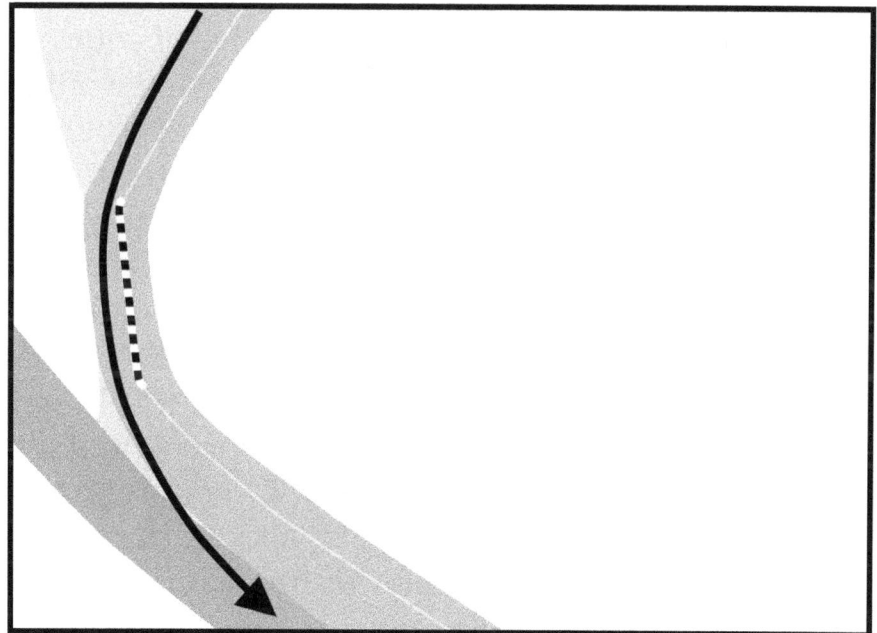

The next series of several right to left corners, which really are just slight steering inputs, is simply a flat open paved area of the infield described by cones and stacks of tires on the left and right sides. Although several straight sections, this is navigated as a curved acceleration run to the entry for the front straight. Determine the best and fastest arc from right to left through it so that you will be at WOT well before you hit the entry apron to the banked front straight, preferably in fourth gear before you meld back onto the main straight, and carry that advantage for better than a mile all the way down and through the Roval. This really depends on the grip of your tires and suspension, so a "one size fits all" advisory doesn't work well. If you can go WOT and manage the up shift between the slight corner segments that is what you can do. But if you upset the balance of your car with a misplaced shift, throttle lift or steering wobble there are numerous stacks of tires to both sides that will wreak havoc upon you if you hit them. Take it easy, be smooth with your technique, and do not lose concentration of the challenge of the moment immediately before you in anticipation and eagerness to get to the front straight.

(Beginner's note: After all of the clearly marked corners, this section can present itself oddly, with a wide open expanse of concrete and asphalt, widely spaced single stacks of tires, and a few orange cones between them, often laid out in a herky jerky angular set up that varies from track day to track day depending on who is placing the cones and tire stacks. Visualize a smooth arc taking advantage of all of the surface between the rows of tires and cones, rather than falling to the temptation of trying to clip closely to the inside tire stacks, which narrows the radius of the corner and thus reduces your exit speed.)

AFTER TURN 17 TO THE FRONT STRAIGHT

As you do your warm up lap, carefully observe the set up of the cones and tire stacks and how they define the segment for Turns 18 through 21. If they describe a smooth and steady arc, you know what to do. But if instead they are configured as shown in the course map on page 13, you confront a subtle nuance that can increase risk of an encounter with a stack of tires, and cost you several miles per hour at entry to the front straight. Observe the geometry of the corner and note that if you make a typically optimized entry to Turn 18, the arc radius for Turn 19 is smaller than it is for Turn 18, while you are at, or at least desire to be, under full acceleration through both corners. That may not present a problem for you. However, a lot of cars can handle full acceleration under cornering load in Turn 18, but then may have to breathe off throttle just a touch before entry to Turn 19 to stay stuck to the pavement. Or, they "back off" from full throttle in Turn 18 so that they can optimize entry to Turn 19... premised upon the driving through Turn 18 that was "tight". That penalizes the driver for almost a mile! Accordingly, consider the potential superiority for your car of adjusting your driving line for a later and wider corner entry to Turn 18 that is focused upon an apex point that is several feet to the right and outside the tire stack on the left edge, but orients you to a tight apex on Turn 19 with a few extra degrees of nose angle towards the left. This wider arc will give you more time on full throttle and thus speed, more safely, so that as you track out from corner exit on Turn 19 you are not as closely skirting the tire stacks to the right. The relatively few extra feet of travel from the wider arc should be more than amply recovered and exceeded by the higher speed carried into and all the way down the front straight. The little right-left "wiggle" at the end of the segment is then of almost no consequence as you describe a very gentle left to right input to put yourself on the front straight, and the banking comfortably collects your right to left adjustment to your chosen driving line.

AFTER TURN 17 TO THE FRONT STRAIGHT

The lead car probably wants to be about two feet more to the right, and with a bit more angle of entry towards the left. Otherwise the driver must input additional steering and the stacks of tires ahead can be more of a factor than you desire.

No caption needed here. Give it all there is, until there is no more!

Merge to front straight. Right side suspension and tires are working hard here.

Enter front straight low and smoothly track up to your predetermined driving line. Do not meander left and right searching for a driving line as you hurtle down the straight at full throttle.

Track Exit

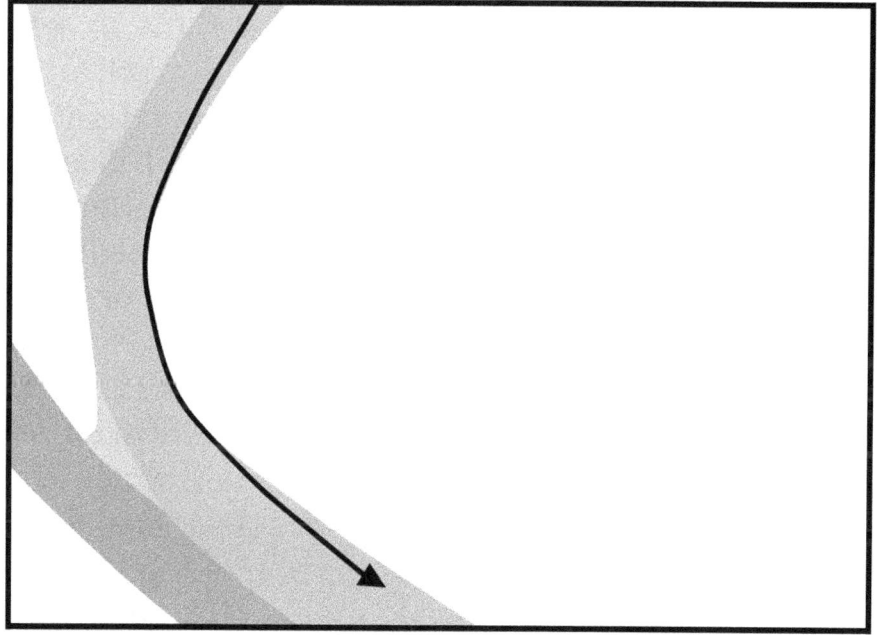

Following your exit from Turn 17, get your arm out of the window to give the track exit signal, move left off the driving line, and proceed quickly through the corner and then left into the exit lane towards the hot pit. The corner exit speed here is slow enough that you should have plenty of room and time to move left even with a pursuing car close behind. (Making a pass on this narrow section is not advised, unless the car in front of you is exiting and cleared the driving line in front of you.)

You should as the exiting car keep up your speed until you meld left into the entry to the hot pit, respecting following drivers that are going as fast as possible for entry to the long front straight. This hot pit entry is usually marked with a line or lines of orange cones curving from right to left, that direct you in a channel to the hot pit lane. Once in the hot pit lane drop your speed safely and proceed smoothly to the exit tunnel located about mid track on the left, and pull under the stands, emerging into the paddock area near the refueling station, to return to your garage or open staging area.

Be immediately wary of pedestrian traffic that can potentially step into your path from either side as you exit the tunnel before you enter the paddock. That area has concession and food stands, restrooms, stairways to the roof top viewing stands over the race day garages, etc., and with all the surrounding noise and distraction it is not uncommon for someone to be more focused on their plate of jalapeno laced nachos, dashing to the restroom, or even unsupervised children bored with watching the cars roar by on the track and playing, and oblivious to the dangers of where they are walking or even running, just at the point in time where your intense focus on driving this challenging circuit is letting up, and the shadow and light that plays upon entry and exit from the tunnel obscures you to pedestrians and they from you, as you come through the narrow field of view in the tunnel. It is always bad form to pull in to your garage space with cheese, chips and peppers on the windscreen and somebody chasing you on foot from behind.

Distinguishing Characteristics

The distinguishing characteristics of Auto Club Speedway are not to be found in dramatic elevation changes or off camber turns, but rather in the 75 foot wide, 11 degree banked front straight of 3100 feet feeding into the 14 degree banked oval NASCAR Turns 1 and 2 (the "Roval"), sustained maximum braking segments with multiple gear downshifts, high speed lateral inertial weight transfers, and the comparatively high overall speeds attained for road cars. Exiting the Roval the driver carries down the 3 degree banked back straight not quite half way, about 1,100 feet, then turns into the flat infield course section, winds back and forth through 130.7 acres, and eventually connects into the front straight at the exit of the NASCAR Turn 4.

While the course guide says the configuration is 21 turns, my perspective is that a chicane or horseshoe hairpin should be counted as 1, and not 2 corners, that the Roval is one big beast...

but not two corners... and thus while reasonable minds can and do differ, for a driver it really presents as closer to 13 or 14 corners, and eight to ten segments for analysis. Described another way, part of the challenge is that this circuit throws corners at you in "bunches", and you have to carefully analyze your optimal approach to negotiating your way through them.

The 1121 foot base elevation does not vary on this flat course by more than a few feet, and most of that is encountered on the banked track surface of the front straight and the Roval. No bulldozer created humps or swales to create an artificial elevation change on this track. The course alternates hard accelerating high speed runs with sharp double 90 degree compound corners, and hairpin corners, at the end of long straights that place importance on sustained extreme braking and multiple heel/toe gear drops on entry to Turns 3, 10, and 13, hard sustained acceleration with multiple gear up shifts from Turns 6, 10, and 21, multiple rapid weight transfers in Turns 3-4, the chicane of Turns 7-8, Turns 11-12 and Turns 13-14 , and severe challenge to the cooling of the engine, cooling of the steering and cooling of the brakes.

Conclusion

Auto Club Speedway's auto competition course with the Roval is a very interesting track experience, combining brute power with very sophisticated braking, down shifting and weight transfer challenges. It is a circuit that is brutally demanding on brakes and cooling systems, especially in the summer months, and can be one of the most technically challenging for car control when combined with high speeds. Auto Club Speedway is a "must do" for the experienced track enthusiast. For the novice driver this should not be the first track they attempt to drive unless they are with a reputable sponsor group and you have formal instruction with in car instructors. For both novice and intermediate level drivers the circuit might be better experienced the first time as a passenger with an instructor behind the wheel, and then with an instructor in the right side seat. Even for advanced level drivers coming to Auto Club Speedway for the first time it is strongly recommended to have a ride with an instructor for orientation to the Roval.

Reflect for just a moment, that all of the driving decisions described above, and more, will transpire in a single lap, compressed into less than two minutes, as contrasted to the considerably longer time that it took you to read a summary description. And this will be repeated ten to twelve times in a single session of HPDE driving, without pause or respite physically, mentally or emotionally. And you will have four, five or even six sessions available to you in a single day of driving.

Closing Note on Driving Lines

There is much more to determining the optimal driving line (and braking inception points, corner turn in points, corner apex points, track out points, etc.) than just an exercise in geometry on a flat road map. Because that is only the starting place for developing the "best" driving line for you.

Track conditions will influence your evaluation of the line to take. What is the weather? Is it cold or warm? Is it dry, humid or even wet? What is the condition of the surface in any given location of the track? Is the camber positive, negative or neutral? Is the surface ascending or descending?

The car you are driving will influence your evaluation of the line to take. What type of car are you driving, how heavy is it, what is the weight balance of the car, where are the drive wheels, what type of suspension (springs/ dampers/ control arms/ camber adjustments/ anti sway bars/ strut towers/ bushings), what type of tire and tire compound, inflation pressure, tire size, how much horsepower/torque, what type of slip differential, what type and size of brakes/brake fluid/pads do you have?

Who is driving will influence the evaluation of the line to take. What is your experience, what are your skill sets, how familiar are you with the particular track, what is your physical condition, are you mentally sharp and focused today?

Now add to this the fact that many of these factors are variables that change throughout the course of the day, indeed some of them through the course of a single session. Accordingly the purpose of the driving lines presented in this guide are to give a general orientation for you to become familiar with the track and then promptly develop your own before you begin to push your personal envelope that day. Obviously, novices should not be "pushing" anything other than the priority of having a fun safe day by staying well under the limits of performance for the track, the car, and themselves. This guide is not written to teach driving. There are many other excellent books that address technique, and excellent driving and racing schools. I encourage you to explore both to the fullest of your ability to do so, as they will enhance both your safety and enjoyment of high performance driving.

Track Checklist

Minimum Required of All Run Groups

- ❑ Helmet. Snell rated SA 2000 or better. Motorcycle helmets are not acceptable.
- ❑ Tech Inspection form
- ❑ Car Numbers – required on both sides of the car and rear, a minimum of eight inches high – this can be with blue painter's masking tape – any self adhering but removable and re usable numbers, vinyl or magnetic, must not peel off at high speed
- ❑ Tow hook installed (preferred) or tow point clearly established
- ❑ Long sleeve cotton shirt and full waist to ankle cotton pants (Cotton or Nomex clothing ONLY. No leather or synthetics allowed. This includes underwear).
- ❑ Closed toe shoes, preferably with a thinner sole for improved pedal feel, cotton socks
- ❑ Torque wrench, lug nut socket that fits your wheels
- ❑ Tire pressure gauge

Highly Recommended for Intermediate and Advanced Groups

- ❑ Driving Suit of not less than two layers, preferably three layers, fire resistant Nomex

- ❏ Race Driving gloves
- ❏ Race Driving shoes
- ❏ Nomex socks, undergarments, balaclava
- ❏ Face shield for helmet
- ❏ Fire Extinguisher, fixed within reach of seated and belted driver
- ❏ Neck brace, collar or Hans Device
- ❏ Racing seat or bucket
- ❏ Properly installed harness system of five points or more, three inch or more belt width.

Optional Supplies

For the Driver:

- ❏ Drinking water or electrolyte drinks. No alcohol drinks permitted on track site at any time. No smoking anywhere in the garage or pit areas.
- ❏ Hat – for Sun
- ❏ Sunglasses
- ❏ Sun Screen
- ❏ Folding chair
- ❏ EZ-UP Canopy
- ❏ Hand Soap/clean wipes
- ❏ Ice chest
- ❏ First aid kit
- ❏ Map/directions/phone number of hotel
- ❏ Map/directions/phone number of track
- ❏ Camera
- ❏ Camcorder/mount

For the Car:

- ❏ Extra Brake pads
- ❏ Brake fluid – one bottle
- ❏ Engine Oil – two quarts
- ❏ Power steering fluid – one bottle
- ❏ Coolant-Radiator- one gallon
- ❏ Distilled Water – Radiator- one gallon
- ❏ Duct tape – one roll
- ❏ Painter's tape – one roll
- ❏ Glass cleaner – You will kill some bugs on your way to the track. You may collect rubber streaks from "marbles" and more bugs on the track
- ❏ Brake Bleeder line and collector bottle
- ❏ Hose Clamps- assorted sizes
- ❏ Zip ties – one dozen
- ❏ Work gloves, heat resistant
- ❏ Jack – as light a weight yet strong as you can find
- ❏ Two foot long wood 2" X 4" stud
- ❏ Jack stands (2) minimum
- ❏ Jumper Cables or Jump starter box
- ❏ Service manual
- ❏ Other tools (sockets, wrenches, pliers, screwdrivers, allen keys...)
- ❏ Utility knife, multipurpose tool, scissors
- ❏ Grease
- ❏ Paper Towels – one roll
- ❏ Clean rags - six
- ❏ Trash bags - two

- ❏ Run Flat aerosol cans
- ❏ Tie Wraps
- ❏ Stopwatch
- ❏ Race tires and wheels, one set
- ❏ Spare tire
- ❏ Tire pyrometer
- ❏ Flashlight
- ❏ Funnel for oil
- ❏ Gloves – disposable
- ❏ Air compressor for tires
- ❏ Data logger
- ❏ Transponder
- ❏ Two way radio/walkie-talkie set
- ❏ Bucket
- ❏ Chamois
- ❏ Bug cleaner/degreaser
- ❏ Mild car soap
- ❏ Car sponge

Tech Inspection Form

Driver: _____ Date: _____

Make: _____ Model: _____

Year: _____ Color: _____ Stock or Modified: _____

Note: If you are self-teching your car, it is your obligation to physically check every item on this form. Do not assume your lugs are tight, re-torque them to make sure. This checklist is for your safety and the safety of the others on the track with you, and should not be dismissed as a formality. If the item is "good" mark with a check. If it is not, write "NO" and call it to the attention of the registrar, and support will be found to assist you to address the issue. After teching your car, you must sign the bottom of the form (in both places if you're self teching), which indicates that you have, in good faith, checked every item on this form. Please bring this form with you to the track, or you'll have to do a new tech at the track before you will be allowed on the track, possibly missing your first run group.

WHEEL and TIRES
Street Tires:
❏ More than 2/32" of tread?
Race Tires:
❏ Good condition/no cording?
❏ Cuts or other defects?
❏ All lugs present and torqued?
❏ Hub/Center-caps removed?

ENGINE
❏ Any fluid leaks?
❏ Wires/hoses secured ?
❏ Throttle return springs tight?
❏ Radiator overflow OK?
❏ Battery properly secured?
❏ Battery terminals covered
    (rubber boots / duct tape OK)?
❏ Fluid lines OK?

BRAKES
❏ Pedal pressure firm?
❏ Fluid level correct?
❏ Lines OK?
❏ Brakes lights working?
❏ Pads more than 5mm?
❏ Rotors OK (no cracks, etc.)?

STEERING & SUSPENSION
❏ Wheel bearings OK (no play)?
❏ Steering tight?

BODY
❏ Gas cap OK?
❏ Body panels secure?

SAFETY EQUIPMENT
❏ Helmet approved?
    (Snell 2000 or newer, M or SA)
❏ Seats secure?
❏ Long sleeve cotton shirt?
❏ Closed-toed shoes?
❏ Seatbelts properly installed?

APPROVED SEATBELTS
The following systems are approved: (Please check one)
❏ OEM 3-Point
❏ 5 or 6-Point
4-Point*
*All 4-Point systems must pass fech at the event.
*4-Point Belts inspected by:_____

Note: Mark each line with a check (✓) if that item is OK; write "NO" if that item is not OK.

Print Name: _____ Signature: _____

Dedication

This book is dedicated to the many people that this adventure in high performance driving has brought me together with, past-present-future, and that I would never have otherwise met. The fraternity of drivers at HPDE has been steadfastly friendly and supportive in these early years, with helpful advice in learning courses and driving, shouldering jacks and pushing cars on and off trailers, even sharing parts and tools when necessary. All with a genuine shared enthusiasm for the sport, and a concern for the safety and well being of each other on and off the track. I hope with this effort to give back to our growing community a resource that will encourage safety, responsibility and development of skills so that all involved, both experienced and novice, will stay safe and well as they pursue their passion for driving.

Acknowledgement

Many thanks to Steve Staveley, former Regional Executive of the California Sports Car Club, and to Jerry Griffin, competition driver and Porsche Club driving instructor, for their generous time in reviewing this work and providing their excellent expert insights, perspectives and suggestions for additional elements to include or emphasize in this text. One cannot have more knowledgeable support than from those who have years of experience teaching others to drive this complex track. And thanks for their enthusiasm and encouragement not only for this title, but to continue with the series of titles addressing the excitement of experiencing high performance driving education on America's road racing circuits. Their responsiveness and commitment of time, experience and energy to deliver the depth of thought and reflection necessary, on top of their already crowded schedules, is characteristic of the comraderie within the fraternity of drivers, as well as the desire so many of us have to participate in communicating to the community of enthusiasts detailed information to help everyone prepare better for safe, enjoyable days of motorsports.

Photo courtesy of Sammy Davis Photography–Los Angeles, CA

About the Author

Edwin Reeser is just another one of the millions of motorsports enthusiasts, who devotes entirely too much time, energy and funds to the passion of high performance driving. You too will have reached this point when 1) you won't supersize your french fries order for a few additional pennies but think nothing of spending another $1,500 for a high flow exhaust, 2) accept the logic of the racer's adage "if you are under control you are not going fast enough", and 3) have no emotional reaction to substantial cosmetic or mechanical damage to your car, when you formerly would have had hysterical upset from a door ding, other than concern over how long will it take before you can get back on the track.

Other Race Track Attack Guides from Sericin Publishing released in 2010:

Laguna Seca - Monterey, California

Willow Springs International Motorsports Park - "Big Willow" - Rosamond, California

Buttonwillow Raceway Park - Race #13 Clockwise - Buttonwillow, California

Reno Fernley Raceway Park - Configuration A - Fernley, Nevada

Thunderhill Raceway Park, Willows, California

Track guides in preparation for future release:

Sears Point Raceway, Sonoma, California

Las Vegas Motor Speedway, Las Vegas, Nevada

Spring Mountain Motor Sports Ranch, Pahrump, Nevada

Willow Springs International Motorsports Park - Streets of Willow, Rosamond, California

For more information go to:
www.RaceTrackGuides.com

www.ingramcontent.com/pod-product-compliance
Lightning Source LLC
Chambersburg PA
CBHW072159100426
42738CB00011BA/2479